PETS' GUIDES

Caring for Your Birds

Isabel Thomas

Heinemann
LIBRARY
Chicago, Illinois

Edited by James Benefield and Brynn Baker
Designed by Cynthia Akiyoshi
Picture research by Tracy Cummins
Production by Victoria Fitzgerald
Originated by Capstone Global Library Ltd
Printed in the United States of America in
Eau Claire, Wisconsin. 102014 008569RP

Library of Congress Cataloging-in-Publication Data

Thomas, Isabel, 1979- author.
  Beaky's guide to caring for your bird / Isabel
Thomas.
       pages cm.—(Pets' guides)
  Summary: "In this book, Beakie the Budgie
reveals how readers should go about choosing
a pet bird, what supplies they will need, how to
make a new pet bird feel at home, and how to
properly care for a pet bird, including feeding,
exercising, and keeping a bird cage clean. Text is
accompanied by clear, labeled photographs to
further reinforce key concepts, and the use of an
animal narrator also allows the book to be used
to teach perspective"— Provided by publisher.
  Includes bibliographical references and index.

ISBN 978-1-4846-0259-1 (hardcover)
ISBN 978-1-4846-0266-9 (paperback)
ISBN 978-1-4846-0282-9 (eBook PDF)
1. Budgerigar—Juvenile literature. 2. Cage birds—
Juvenile literature. I. Title.
  SF473.B8
  636.6'8—dc23   2013040426

Acknowledgments
We would like to thank the following for permission
to reproduce photographs: Alamy: © Marmaduke
St. John, 19; Capstone Library: Karon Dubke, 7, 11,
12, 14, 20, 23, 26; Getty Images: Andreas Arnold,
5; Shutterstock: Edoma, 9, Sarycheva Olesia, 16;
Superstock: Belinda Images, 24, imagebroker.net,
front cover; Design Elements Shutterstock: iBird,
Picsfive, R-studio

We would like to thank Les Rance for his
assistance in the preparation of this book.

Every effort has been made to contact copyright
holders of material reproduced in this book. Any
omissions will be rectified in subsequent printings
if notice is given to the publisher.

Contents

Some words are shown in bold, **like this**. You can find out what they mean by looking in the glossary.

Do You Want Pet Birds?

G'day! I'm Beaky the budgie, and this book is all about birds like me! Did you know that some birds make great pets? Our colorful feathers and happy birdsong will brighten up your home. Some of us can even talk to you!

Before getting a pet bird, be sure you can look after me properly. I'll need a safe, clean place to live, food and water, things to play with, company, and **vet** care if I get sick or injured. Care for me well and I'll quickly become your best friend!

Choosing Your Birds

Budgies like me are the most popular pet birds. I'm not surprised – we're beautiful! Cockatiels, zebra finches, and canaries also make great family pets. Some birds will happily hop on to your hand or sit on your shoulder. Others do not like to be handled.

I feel lonely when I'm kept on my own. If you would like to keep budgies or zebra finches, buy at least two birds. Then we'll always have company. It's best to get two boy birds or two girl birds.

Before you buy a bird, ask where it came from. I am happy to live with people because I was born in **captivity**. Never buy or keep birds that have been taken from the wild.

Me when I was little

Animal shelters and **rescue centers** are the best places to get new pets. You can also buy birds at pet stores or from a good **breeder**. It is best to choose young birds, or birds that are already **hand tamed**.

Getting Ready

Now it's time to go shopping. Make sure you have everything you need before you bring me home. I can't sleep in your bed! I need plenty of space to stretch my wings and to keep fit by flying. My dream home is an **aviary**.

Pet birds can also be kept in a wire cage. Make sure you choose the largest one possible. Different types of birds need different cages. Ask a vet or a bird expert for advice. If the bars are too far apart, your new pets could escape. They could get their beak, wings, or feet trapped.

Don't forget the furniture! Pet birds need several **perches** at different heights. Look for specially cleaned tree branches in pet stores. I'll also need lots of toys, so I never get bored. You don't have to wait until it's my birthday!

Beaky's Budgie Shopping List:

- an aviary or wire cage
- perches the right size for my feet
- budgie food
- food and water containers
- paper to line the bottom of my cage
- special bird toys

Welcome Home

Moving can be scary, especially for birds. Help me settle in by picking the perfect place for my cage. My favorite spot is the corner of a warm, light room. I'll enjoy watching you play, but I'll also feel safe.

Please don't
put my cage:

✗ next to a window. I don't like **drafts** or
bright sunshine.

✗ near a radiator or heater

✗ on the floor

✗ near a TV or radio

✗ in or near the kitchen. Cooking **fumes** can
make me ill.

✗ in a room where strong-smelling things like
hairspray, perfume, glue, or paints are used

✗ in a room where somebody smokes.

Feeding Time

You can buy special bird food from pet stores. Pellets are like a perfect packed lunch, and they help me to stay healthy. Ask for help to choose my food. I need fresh, cold water to drink all the time. Also, seeds make a delicious treat!

Budgies can't eat all fruit and vegetables. Check out the list on page 28. However, I like to nibble fresh food every day. How about making it a game by hiding small pieces of fruit and vegetables in my cage? Wash everything well and take out any pits.

Cleaning My Home

I need a clean home to stay healthy. I can't clean out my cage, so I'm relying on you! Clear away **stale** food, and wash out my water container every day. Change the paper at the bottom of my cage to get rid of any droppings.

You will need to **disinfect** the whole cage every week. Remember to clean my toys and perches, too. Perches made from tree branches can be replaced if they get too dirty to wipe clean.

Handling and Exercise

Cockatiels and budgies can learn to perch on your hand. Start by putting your hand in our cage to offer a tasty treat. Move slowly and quietly so I don't get frightened. Next, try holding out a perch or finger for me to hop on to.

When I am hand tamed, let me out of my
cage every day. Pet birds need to exercise
by flying around a safe room. Keep windows
and doors closed, and watch me carefully
so I don't nibble anything dangerous. Cover
windows and mirrors so I don't fly into them
by mistake. Ouch!

Grooming and Care

I need a bath every day to keep my feathers clean. Give me a bowl of shallow water and I'll do the hard work! You can even give pet birds a shower by spraying clean water from a **mister**.

Just like your fingernails, my beak never stops growing. Chewing special wooden toys will stop my beak from getting too long. Please don't let me nibble painted wood, furniture, or your toys. They could poison me.

Visiting the Vet

Take me to visit a vet when I first come to live with you. I'll need a check-up every year. The vet can help you to care for me, make sure I'm healthy, and trim my beak and nails.

Birds can't tell you when they feel ill. If you spot any of these sickness signs, take me to the vet right away:

- I've fluffed up my feathers
- I'm quiet or sleepy
- I'm fatter or thinner than usual
- I'm eating or drinking less than usual
- my droppings are runny
- I'm sneezing or coughing
- I'm limping
- my beak or eyes are crusty

Vacation Care

When you go on vacation, ask a friend or neighbor to visit me every day. They'll need to fill my food and water, and keep my cage clean. Tell them what sickness signs to look out for.

We are best friends now, so I'll miss you while you're away. Remember to tell me all about your vacation when you get back. I love it when you talk to me. I might even start to chatter back!

Budgie Facts

- The proper name for budgies is budgerigars.

- The first budgies came from Australia.

- Wild budgies are always green and yellow.

- Pet budgies can be hundreds of different colors and patterns.

- Pet budgies can live for up to 15 years. Most live for about 8 years.

- Rhubarb, avocado, and chocolate are poisonous to budgies.

- Like all birds, budgies are scared of animals like cats and dogs. A pet bird might not be a good choice if you already have other pets.

Beaky's Top Tips

- Choose lots of toys for your pet birds, and swap them around so we don't get bored. We like swings, ladders, and mirrors for **preening**. We enjoy toys we can chew or ones with bells or chimes.

- Try making your own bird toys. Use safe materials such as cardboard tubes, dried pasta, sucker sticks, and clean shoelaces.

- Don't worry if I try to tear my toys apart – it's part of the fun!

- Play with me lots. You can even teach me games such as climbing your fingers, hide and seek, or ringing a bell.

- Seeds and popcorn are special treats. But I shouldn't have them too often because they are fattening!

Glossary

animal shelter place for animals that have no home

aviary room-sized cage for keeping birds in

breeder person who helps animals to have babies in an organized way

captivity kept by humans instead of living in the wild

disinfect clean something with special chemicals to kill harmful germs

draft cool breeze inside a building from an open door or window

fume any gas or vapor that has a strong smell or is dangerous to breathe in

hand tamed used to being handled

mister bottle with a sprayer attached to create a mist

perch when a bird rests on something, or the object they rest on

preen when a bird cleans its feathers using its beak

rescue center organization that rescues animals that are lost, injured, or not being taken care of properly

stale not fresh and not good to eat

vet person trained to care for sick or injured animals

Find Out More

Books

Alderton, David. *How to Look After Your Budgie*.
Armadillo Books, 2013.

Morgan, Sally. Pets Plus: *Birds*.
Mankato, Minn.: Smart Apple Media, 2013.

Websites

Learn more about caring for birds at:
http://humanesociety.org/animals/pet_birds

Discover more about birds at:
http://bbc.co.uk/nature/life/Bird

Index